STARS OF THE ROCK 'N' ROLL HIGHWAY

STARS *of the* ROCK 'N' ROLL HIGHWAY

VICTORIA MICKLISH PASMORE

Plum Street Publishers, Inc.

LITTLE ROCK

Published 2015 by Plum Street Publishers, Inc.,
2701 Kavanaugh Boulevard, Suite 202, Little Rock, Arkansas 72205
www.plumstreetpublishers.com

Book and cover design by Liz Lester
(Cover photo of Conway Twitty courtesy of Joni Jenkins Riels; photo of
Wanda Jackson copyright Bear Family Records.)

First Edition
Manufactured in the United States of America
10 9 8 7 6 5 4 3 2 1   PB (ISBN 0–978–0-9905971–5-5)

LIBRARY OF CONGRESS CONTROL NUMBER: 2015947463

The paper used in this publication meets the minimum requirements of
the American National Standards for Information Sciences—Permanence
of Paper for Printed Library Materials, ANSI / NISO Z39.48–1992.

To my parents,
John and Mari Lou Pasmore,
who saw the birth of rock 'n' roll;
Peter,
who shares my passion for the music;
Elvis Presley,
my first rock 'n' roll love;
and my son David,
who also loves "The King"

CONTENTS

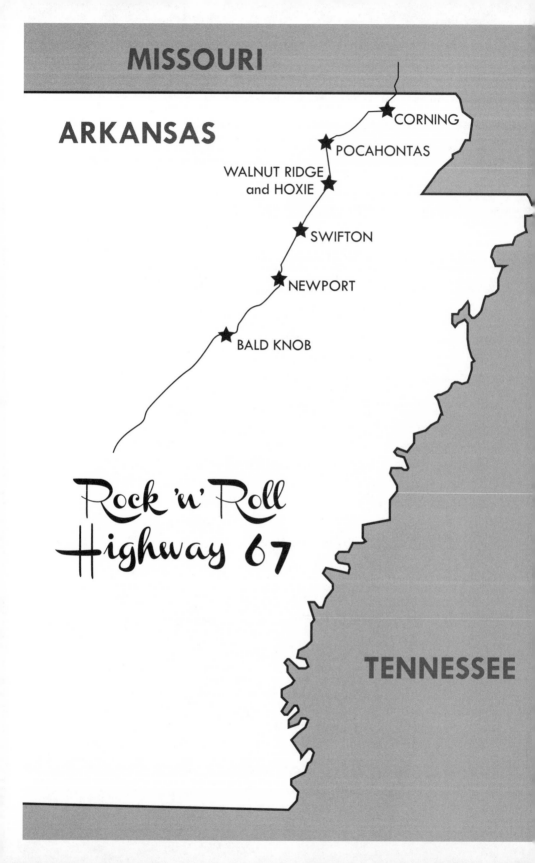

INTRODUCTION

If the birthplace of Rock 'n' Roll is Memphis, Tennessee, it certainly spent its adolescence in northeast Arkansas. Highway 67 runs 111 miles from Newport, Arkansas, in Jackson County, to the Arkansas–Missouri border. It is here that the first rock 'n' rollers staged their early performances and honed their skills, playing the small towns that dotted this two-lane highway. These young musicians and singers performed their music in school gyms and cafeterias, honky-tonks, and clubs that dotted Highway 67 with such colorful names as Bloody Bucket, Silver Moon, Porky's Rooftop, and Bob King's King of Clubs. They even played on the roof of the Skylark Drive In Theater.

Most of these performers had similar family backgrounds. They were Southern, rural, and poor. They grew up listening to Southern gospel, rhythm and blues, and country music sung by the black and white voices around them. Several of them were mentored by African-American musicians. By combining the sounds of the music they grew up listening to, these performers produced a brand new sound. Young rural teenagers were the first to hear this new music. They looked up, took notice, and became its first fans. In the early days of rock 'n' roll the music was known as *rockabilly*. This term was originally dismissive, intending to make fun of its Southern roots. As it turned out, this music appealed not only to the young Southerners who created it and those who became its early fans, but to the world as a whole; it created a musical revolution. Later this music would be called *rock 'n' roll*. Rock 'n' roll not only changed the musical landscape but also influenced popular culture.

Many music historians say that rock 'n' roll was born at Sun Records at Memphis. Originally Memphis Recording Service, it was founded by Sam Phillips in 1952. During this time, many small independent record labels sprang up around the South. Aspiring artists, or those who were just curious to know how they sounded, could walk in the door, pay their money, and record a song. Originally known for his work with African-American blues artists, Phillips recorded such greats as Howlin' Wolf, B.B. King, Rufus Thomas, and Junior Parker. He ran a production studio, Sun Studio, as well as a record label, Sun Records.

In the early days of Sun Records, Phillips said, "If I could find a white man who had the Negro sound and Negro feel, I could make a million bucks." In 1954, he found that man: Elvis Presley. Working with Phillips, Elvis and his band combined the sounds of country, rhythm and blues, and Southern gospel. Rock 'n' roll was born. Inspired by this new sound and seeking their own musical fortunes, other young musicians such as Johnny Cash, Jerry Lee Lewis, Carl Perkins, and Billy Lee Riley also launched their careers at Sun.

Not too far away, in Trumann, Arkansas, another recording company opened. Arlen Vaden founded Vaden Records, originally a mail-order company offering gospel music. Vaden scouted the musicians who performed along Highway 67 and launched the recording careers of such early rockers as Larry Donn, Joyce Green, Bobby Brown, and Teddy Redell.

The innovative sound created by the early rockabilly artists evolved into rock 'n' roll. This ever-changing musical style is as popular today as it was when it emerged more than sixty years ago. Although rockabilly waned in popularity, it enjoyed a revival in the 1980s. Fans in the United States and particularly in Europe, eager to hear the founding rockabilly artists, gave these artists an "encore career" when most people their age have retired. It is interesting to note that many of today's rock 'n' roll greats give credit to the early rockabilly artists as their musical inspiration.

In 2009 the Arkansas General Assembly named Highway 67 the Rock 'n' Roll Highway (or Rock 'n' Roll Highway 67) in recognition of its importance in the history of rock 'n' roll music and culture.

Let's take a trip down Highway 67 and meet some of the performers who gave the Rock 'n' Roll Highway its name. Listen carefully, and you may hear the music.

—Victoria Micklish Pasmore
May 2015

Elvis Presley

ELVIS ARON PRESLEY was born in 1935 in a two-room house built by his father, Vernon, in Tupelo, Mississippi. His twin brother, Jesse Garron, died at birth. Elvis was an only child. Because she lost one son, Elvis's mother Gladys would be very protective of him.

Music was always important to the Presleys. Elvis and his family sang Southern gospel music in church. He grew up listening to rhythm and blues sung by his African-American neighbors. He listened to country music on the radio. For his twelfth birthday, Gladys took Elvis to Tupelo Hardware and bought him a guitar. Some people say he wanted a bicycle. Others say he wanted a BB gun. But that guitar was probably the most important gift Elvis would ever receive.

Looking for better opportunities, the Presley family moved to the city of Memphis, Tennessee when Elvis was thirteen. Elvis still listened to the music he loved. In Memphis, he had the opportunity to see live concerts by famous gospel quartets. He listened to the rhythm and blues he loved on Beale Street, where he also bought his unusual-looking clothes.

In 1954, he went to Sun Studio and met Sam Phillips. He made his first record, "My Happiness," for his mother. A few months later, Phillips called Elvis back to record more songs. Elvis recorded "That's All Right," which combined the sounds of country, gospel, and rhythm and blues, creating a new sound called rock 'n' roll.

In his early career, Elvis performed at numerous clubs along the Rock 'n' Roll Highway. He played at the Newport Armory, Porky's Rooftop, the Silver Moon, Bob King's King of Clubs, and the Swifton High School gym. He also performed shows in Bono, Jonesboro, Nettleton, Leachville, Helena, Little Rock, and West Memphis.

As a young performer, Elvis scandalized many adults with his wiggling movements on stage, causing many parents to forbid their children from watching or listening. But Elvis became more and more popular and eventually left Sun for RCA Records and became an international star. His early hits include "Hound Dog," "Heartbreak Hotel," and "All Shook Up." Elvis later became a popular movie star and continued to record and tour until his death in 1977 at age forty-two.

One of the most influential musicians of the twentieth century, Elvis was inducted into the Rock and Roll Hall of Fame, Country Music Hall of Fame, Gospel Music Hall of Fame, and Rockabilly Hall of Fame. He was awarded three Grammy Awards, including the Lifetime Achievement Award.

Did You Know?

- Elvis never learned to read music and failed music in high school.

- Elvis's home, Graceland, is the second-most visited private house in the world.

- Elvis named his airplane after his daughter Lisa Marie, who is also a singer.

- His appearance on *The Ed Sullivan Show* drew a record TV audience of 60 million viewers. The History Channel selected this episode as one of the days that changed America.

- "That's All Right" is recognized as the first official rock 'n' roll song.

Sonny Burgess

SONNY BURGESS was born Albert Austin Burgess outside Newport, Arkansas in 1931. He had two brothers and three sisters. Sonny and his family lived on a farm. When he was a child, Sonny listened to a country radio program called the *Grand Ole Opry*. He also heard rhythm and blues on WDIA, a radio station broadcast from Memphis, Tennessee.

After graduating from high school, Sonny started his first band. It was called The Drifting Cowboys. Later, they became The Rocky

Road Ramblers, playing along Highway 67 until Sonny joined the army in 1951. In 1954 he returned to Newport and reunited the band as The Moonlighters, after Newport's Silver Moon Club.

Sonny's band soon became popular for its music. The audience also liked how the band members moved on stage. They would slide across the floor. They would jump into the audience. They did acrobatics onstage and even formed a human pyramid. The crowd went wild!

Sonny and his band often played with Elvis Presley along the Rock 'n' Roll Highway. Elvis liked their sound and suggested they see Sam Phillips, who owned Sun Studio. Phillips took the group on, advising them to expand the band and rename it Sonny Burgess and the Pacers, a name they still use today. Their first record, recorded in 1956, was "We Wanna Boogie." The flip side was a song called "Red-Headed Woman." Other early hits included "Ain't Got a Thing," "Thunderbird" and "My Bucket's Got a Hole in It."

Sonny has been named to the Rock and Roll Hall of Fame and, along with the Pacers, to the Rockabilly Hall of Fame. Today, Sonny still calls Newport, Arkansas his home. Sonny Burgess and the Legendary Pacers tour all over the U.S. and Europe—and still perform along the Rock 'n' Roll Highway.

Did You Know?

- Sonny has his own radio show, We Wanna Boogie, on KASU in Jonesboro, Arkansas.

- Sonny and his band opened for Elvis four times on the Rock 'n' Roll Highway.

- Sonny has lived in Newport, Arkansas his entire life.

- Sonny became known for his trademark red hair, dyed to match his guitar.

- Teen rocker Ricky Nelson also recorded "My Bucket's Got a Hole in It" at the same time Sonny did.

Billy Lee Riley

BILLY LEE RILEY was born in Pocahontas, Arkansas in 1933. He had eight brothers and sisters. His parents were sharecroppers and were very poor. Billy Lee quit school after just three years to help support his family by picking cotton.

Even as a little boy, Billy Lee loved music. When he was six years old he learned to play the harmonica. He listened to the blues with his African-American friends. When he was ten, his daddy bought him his first guitar. A talented singer and musician, he played guitar, bass, and drums.

In the 1950s, Billy Lee began playing the clubs along Highway 67 (his favorite was Bob King's King of Clubs). On Christmas Day, 1956,

Billy Lee and his wife picked up two hitchhikers. They proved to be Jack Clements and Slim Wallace, prominent figures on the music scene. They were in the process of opening their own recording studio, Fernwood, in Memphis. As a result of this chance meeting, Billy Lee became their first recording artist. Pleased with the record, Clements arranged to have Sun Records release it.

Billy Lee and his band, The Little Green Men, worked as session musicians at Sun, backing up most of the songs the studio recorded in the late 1950s. They also recorded their own releases, notably "Flying Saucers Rock and Roll" and "Red Hot." In the early days at Sun, Billy Lee played bass on Jerry Lee Lewis's recording "Great Balls of Fire" while Lewis played piano on several of Billy Lee's early recordings. In 1957, Sam Phillips chose to promote "Great Balls of Fire" over Lewis's "Red Hot," released the same year. This was a lasting disappointment to Billy Lee. He always believed this decision had a negative impact on his career.

But nothing could keep Billy Lee from playing the music he loved. He continued to record and make music for the rest of his life. In 1977, he was nominated for a Grammy Award. Still rocking, he died in 2009.

Did You Know?

- Music stars Bob Dylan and Bruce Springsteen credit Billy Lee with influencing their own careers. In 1992, Dylan went to Newport to meet Billy Lee and persuade him to open his Little Rock show.

- Billy Lee enlisted in the army at only age fifteen after his sister lied about his age. He said later that he joined the army to have a place to live and something to eat.

- Billy Lee's band performed in costumes made out of billiard table felt. After sweat-soaked performances, the fabric left a green stain on their skin, giving rise to the band's name The Little Green Men.

- Billy Lee was banned from Arkansas State University for climbing on top of the piano and dancing.

- Billy Lee was recognized by the Smithsonian Institution as one of the pioneers of rock 'n' roll.

Wanda Jackson

WANDA LAVONNE JACKSON was born in Maud, Oklahoma in 1937. Her father was a musician and country singer. During the Depression it was especially hard to make a living playing music, so Wanda's father decided to quit the music business. The Jackson family moved from Oklahoma to California when Wanda was four.

Wanda grew up surrounded by music. Wanting to encourage her musical interest, Wanda's daddy played music at home, encouraged her to listen to other musicians, and bought her a guitar when she was only six years old. He also encouraged her to learn piano as well. At age twelve, Wanda and her family moved back to Oklahoma. Music remained a constant through her early years. While still a teenager she won a talent contest at a local radio station. Her prize for winning was her own daily radio program.

Wanda first began performing on the Rock 'n' Roll Highway as a country singer in the 1950s. It was there that she met a young singer named Elvis Presley. After hearing her sing, Elvis suggested that she change her style to rockabilly. Wanda took his advice and became of the few female rockabilly artists. The crowds loved her, and she soon earned her nickname, "The Queen of Rockabilly."

Two of Wanda's biggest hits were "Honey Bop" and "Fujiyama Mama." Over the years, she earned two Grammy nominations and was inducted into the Rock and Roll Hall of Fame.

Today, Wanda still continues to perform her rockabilly songs on tours in the United States and Europe.

Did You Know?

- Wanda dated Elvis Presley briefly in the early 1950s.
- Wanda has recorded with modern rock 'n' roller Jack White.
- Bob Dylan has spoken of her as "an atomic fireball of a lady."
- Wanda's mother helped design her dramatic stage costumes.
- After her 1960 recording of "Let's Have a Party" hit the Top 40, she named her band The Party Timers.

Narvel Felts

ALBERT NARVEL FELTS was born in Keiser, Arkansas in 1938. His father was a sharecropper. When Narvel was fourteen, his family moved to Bernie, Missouri.

As a young boy, Narvel showed an interest in music. At thirteen he traded his BB gun for a secondhand Gene Autry guitar held together by wire. Later he was able to replace it for a new one ordered from the Sears Roebuck catalog. He paid $15.98—equal to about $150 today—for it with money he had earned from picking cotton.

When Narvel was seventeen years old he won his high school talent contest, singing "Baby, Let's Play House." A deejay in the audience heard him sing and offered him a live Saturday afternoon radio show. A year later Narvel found himself auditioning for Sun Records. During this time he was touring along the Rock 'n' Roll Highway with Roy Orbison and Eddy Bond and the Stompers.

With Sun Records focused on Johnny Cash and Jerry Lee Lewis, Narvel began recording on Mercury Records. His first Mercury recordings, "Kiss-A-Me Baby" and "Foolish Thoughts," are considered rockabilly classics.

By the end of the 1960s, rockabilly music had declined in popularity. Like many of the early rockabilly artists, Narvel began performing country music and became one of the top country artists of the 1970s. He had more than seventy hits, including "Reconsider Me," which became the Cash Box 1975 Record of the Year.

Narvel still makes his home in Missouri. He continues to tour internationally, performing at both country and rock 'n' roll venues. His records continue to receive airplay across Europe.

Did You Know?

- Narvel sang the Carl Perkins hit "Blue Suede Shoes" as an encore at his high school talent contest.
- Narvel's nickname is "Narvel the Marvel."
- Narvel's son Bud played as a drummer in Narvel's band until he died in a car wreck at age thirty-one.
- Narvel had eleven Top 20 country hits in the 1970s.
- More than 200 of Narvel's recordings have been released on CD.

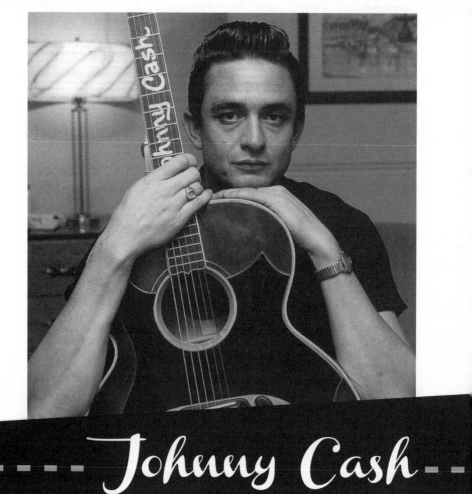

Johnny Cash

JOHNNY CASH was born J.R. Cash in Kingsland, Arkansas in 1932. When he was three years old, he moved with his family to Dyess, Arkansas. Dyess was a community built by the Works Project Administration (WPA) to help needy farm families during the Great Depression. When J.R. was old enough, he worked beside his six brothers and sisters picking cotton.

J.R. Cash grew up surrounded by music. His family listened to country music on the radio. He heard music sung by the field hands as he picked cotton, and his mother taught him gospel songs. When he was a young boy, the family got a piano.

Two events made a lasting impression on young J.R. In 1937, the town of Dyess was flooded. Everyone had to be evacuated by train.

When he grew up he would write a song about the flood called "Five Feet High and Rising." The second event he would always remember was the death of his older brother. Jack was killed in a sawmill accident when J.R. was twelve. It is said that J.R. began writing songs as a way to keep his brother's memory alive.

Like many rockabilly artists, Johnny Cash recorded at Sun Studio in Memphis. Two of his early songs, recorded in 1955, were "Hey Porter" and "Cry, Cry, Cry." Johnny Cash became one of the studio's biggest stars, touring with Elvis and playing along Highway 67 at the Swifton High School gym and King of Clubs. He would go on to become one of the best-selling country music songwriters and singers of all time with such hits as "I Walk the Line," "Folsom Prison Blues," and "Ring of Fire."

Johnny Cash's wide-ranging style allowed him to cross over to many categories. He is one of the few artists to be inducted into the Country Music Hall of Fame, Rock and Roll Hall of Fame, Gospel Music Hall of Fame, and Rockabilly Hall of Fame. He hosted an ABC television show from 1969 to 1971 and was awarded a Grammy Lifetime Achievement Award in 1999.

Johnny Cash died in 2003, just four months after the death of his wife, June Carter Cash.

Did You Know?

- Johnny Cash was known as the "Man in Black" because of his all-black performance wardrobe. Although it lent him a reputation as an outlaw, he chose the clothes for the practical reason that they were easier to keep looking clean on tour.

- Johnny married June Carter of the legendary folk group, The Carter Family, after proposing on stage.

- His children Roseanne Cash and John Carter Cash continue the family tradition as country performers.

- Johnny recorded a live album at Folsom Prison, winning the loyalty of inmates for the rest of his life.

- Johnny was named J.R. at birth, not Johnny. He got the name Johnny in the army, which would not accept initials on the enlistment form.

Conway Twitty

CONWAY TWITTY was born Harold Jenkins in Friars Point, Mississippi in 1933. He was raised in Helena, Arkansas. His father was a riverboat captain.

In Helena, young Harold grew up listening to country music. He also listened to gospel and blues songs. When he was just four years old he picked up his first guitar. By age ten he had his first band, the Phillips County Ramblers. The band occasionally performed on the local radio station on Saturdays.

But Harold Jenkins had another interest besides music. He loved baseball and was a talented player. He wanted to become a professional baseball player when he grew up. This almost happened. After high school he was recruited by the Philadelphia Phillies, but before he could join the team he was drafted into the army.

While in the army, Harold remained interested in music. He formed a band called the Cimarrons to entertain the other soldiers. Returning home from the army, he chose to pursue music instead of baseball. He made this decision after hearing a rising young rockabilly star named Elvis Presley from Sun Records. Harold went to Memphis, where he recorded at Sun. The songs he recorded were not released until later. About that time he began touring with a rockabilly package tour. It was during this time that he performed on the Rock 'n' Roll Highway.

In 1958, Harold left Sun Records. Taking on his new stage name, Conway Twitty, he began recording with MGM, and his career took off. His rock 'n roll successes included such hits as "It's Only Make Believe," "Danny Boy," and "Lonely Blue Boy." He also enjoyed a film career in the 1960s.

During the 1960s Conway began performing country music with such successful hits as "Next in Line," "Hello, Darlin'," and "You've Never Been This Far Before." He was inducted into the Country Music Hall of Fame and Rockabilly Hall of Fame. He continued to record and perform, including a string of duets with Loretta Lynn, until his death in 1993.

Did You Know?

- Conway Twitty got his stage name from two towns: Conway, Arkansas and Twitty, Texas.
- His parents named him Harold after a famous silent film actor, Harold Lloyd.
- His hit song "It's Only Make Believe" was recorded with Elvis's backup band, The Jordanaires.
- Conway had more than forty #1 hits on the country music charts.
- Conway was a lifelong baseball fan and in later year was part owner of the Nashville Sounds, a minor league baseball team.

Barbara Pittman

BARBARA PITTMAN was born in 1938 in Memphis, Tennessee. She was one of twelve children, and her family was very poor. As a child Barbara listened to the music of the big bands, a popular musical style at that time. She also listened to her father play the fiddle.

Barbara's uncle owned a pawn shop on Beale Street in Memphis. Beale Street was already famous for its rhythm and blues music. While visiting her uncle, Barbara would stop to listen to the informal jam sessions. There she saw many talented blues performers, including B.B. King.

Growing up in Memphis had other advantages for Barbara. While just a child she arrived at Sun Studio, ready to make a record. But the eleven-year-old was told to come back when she had grown up and was able to sing. Disappointed, underage—but determined to have a singing career—Barbara began singing at local clubs, earning five dollars a show. She also spent a year touring on a variety show with Western star Lash LaRue.

In 1956 Barbara returned to Memphis and Sun Studio for another try at recording. Owner Sam Phillips saw that she was grown up. Now there was no doubt that she could sing. Phillips signed her to a contract and recorded four singles that were released. Two of her most popular songs were "I Need a Man" and "Two Young Fools in Love."

Barbara began performing with other young rockabilly artists on tours arranged by Sun. Many of those tours took her along Highway 67. While she enjoyed regional success, she never became nationally known. Still, four years of recording at Sun Studio produced material that identifies her as one of the few female rockabilly performers.

After her contract with Sun expired, Barbara left Memphis and moved to California, where she appeared and sometimes sang in teen motorcycle and horror films. She died in 2005.

Did You Know?

- As a child, Barbara attended the same school as Elvis Presley.
- Barbara was the only female singer to receive a recording contract at Sun Records.
- Barbara's mother and Elvis's mother, Gladys Presley, were friends.
- Barbara toured with Jerry Lee Lewis in his *Great Balls of Fire* touring bus.
- Barbara is featured in the Bear Family Records release, *Memphis Belles,* a boxed set featuring female artists who worked for Sun Studio.

Sonny Deckelman

SONNY DECKELMAN was born in Harrisburg, Arkansas in 1933. While many early rockabilly performers came from a farm background, Sonny's family was different. His father was an automobile mechanic, and his mother was a housewife. Sonny was the youngest child in his family. He was raised with three older sisters, and also had a much older half-brother and half-sister.

Like many of the young rockabilly performers, Sonny came from a musical family. His father played the Jew's harp and the French harp, or harmonica. His mother and one of his sisters enjoyed singing. His older cousin Bud Deckelman was a talented singer and musician who would have a recording career in Memphis.

When Sonny was seventeen years old, he and two buddies enlisted in the air force. Sonny was stationed in France for three years. During this time his interest in music grew. He learned to play the drums and guitar. He joined a band as a singer and guitarist.

After his discharge from the air force, Sonny came back to Arkansas. He began singing with bands in the Memphis area and performing on the Rock 'n' Roll Highway. He played at Bob King's King of Clubs, the Silver Moon, and Porky's Rooftop. In 1958 he moved to California to perform but, homesick, returned to Arkansas just three months later. Shortly after his return, he started his own band, The Bop Kings.

Sonny recorded several songs with recording studios in Memphis, including "I've Got Love" and "Born to Lose." "Lonely Street," released in 1964, was especially popular.

Sonny remained in the music business recording and performing. In the 1970s he became a producer at Monument Studios in Nashville. He even had his own record company, Van–Deck Records in Harrisburg. Today, although no longer performing, Sonny still lives in his hometown.

Did You Know?

- Sonny was stationed in Virginia for the first year of his military duty. He was so homesick his father joined him there for the year to keep him company.

- Sonny and his cousin Bud were double cousins. This means two sisters married two brothers.

- Sonny was a frequent guest on the WHBQ television show *Dance Party*, broadcast from Memphis.

- From 1960 to 1969, Sonny was commander of the VFW post in Harrisburg.

- In 2001, Sonny was inducted into the Rockabilly Hall of Fame.

Teddy Redell

TEDDY DELANO RIEDEL was born in 1937 in a small Arkansas town named Quitman. His father was a strawberry farmer. Like many farm families during that time, the Riedels were poor. But they owned something wonderful. The family had an old upright piano. Teddy began taking piano lessons when he was six years old. He first learned to play classical music and then took up ragtime and boogie-woogie. He taught himself hillbilly music and Western swing.

When Teddy was just fifteen years old, he played on KWCB, a

radio station in Searcy, Arkansas. His performance of "Steel Guitar Rag" attracted a flood of requests for more airplay. The station invited him to join a weekly radio show.

As a result of his radio exposure, Teddy began touring in northeast Arkansas and playing the clubs along Highway 67. Soon he was touring the Atlantic Seaboard and had a weekly spot on *The World's Original Jamboree* on WWVA radio in West Virginia.

In the late 1950s, using the stage name Teddy Redell, he recorded several songs for Vaden Records of Trumann, Arkansas. His Vaden recordings included "Knocking on the Backside," "Corinna Corinna," and "I Want to Hold You." His single "Judy" became his most famous song and was later recorded by Elvis.

After a brief stint in the army, Teddy resumed his musical career, playing backup piano. When he became tired of touring, he moved back to Arkansas, where he took up cattle ranching and owned a piano-tuning business.

In the 1970s Teddy began recording again. In the 1980s, during the rockabilly revival, he toured Europe for the first time. He continued performing in Europe and the United States until his death in 2014.

Did You Know?

- Teddy's biggest hit, "Judy," was originally recorded as the B-side of "Can't You See."

- Arlen Vaden of Vaden Records accidentally misspelled Teddy's last name, changing it to Redell. This spelling is still in use today.

- Teddy auditioned for Sam Phillips at Sun in 1957. The songs were never issued and, sadly, are lost.

- The piano player Moon Mullican had a big influence on Teddy and another famous piano player named Jerry Lee Lewis.

- Teddy wrote several songs for popular country singer Sonny James, "The Southern Gentleman."

Carl Perkins

CARL PERKINS was born in Tiptonville, Tennessee in 1932. His parents were sharecroppers. When Carl was six years old, he began picking cotton with his family. He and his two brothers each made fifty cents a day. This money helped feed the family.

While Carl and his family picked cotton, they listened as the African-American field hands sang gospel songs as they worked. When they had free time, his family listened to country music on the radio. In church, Carl sang gospel songs.

Because music was such a big part of Carl's life, it was only natural that he wanted to make his own music. One day, Carl asked his daddy for a guitar. Because they didn't have the money for a real guitar, his daddy took a broomstick and cigar box and fashioned a homemade guitar for his son. Later on, Carl's father was able to buy a used guitar from a neighbor.

Carl had an adult friend named John Westbrook. "Uncle John," as Carl called him, was an African-American musician he knew from the cotton fields. Uncle John encouraged young Carl to play guitar and sing and even gave him musical advice. By the time Carl was fourteen years old, he wrote his first song. Soon after that, he and his brothers began playing and singing locally. They even performed on the radio.

One day Carl Perkins heard Elvis on the radio and decided he needed to go to Memphis and meet Sam Phillips. Like many other rockabilly artists, he recorded at Sun Studio. He also toured with Elvis and Johnny Cash along the Rock 'n' Roll Highway. One place they played together was The King of Clubs.

One night, Carl, Elvis, and Johnny Cash were performing a show at Parkin, Arkansas, near Memphis, when they heard a boy scold his girlfriend for scuffing his suede shoes. Although accounts differ, many say that that night, Carl wrote the lyrics to "Blue Suede Shoes" on a paper bag. He recorded it in December 1955. It was featured on country, pop, and rhythm and blues playlists and became a #2 hit.

Carl also had hits with "Matchbox" and "Dixie Fried." Although he was overshadowed in the U.S. by Elvis Presley and other artists, he toured overseas and found enthusiastic audiences. He was a regular on *The Johnny Cash Show* and continued to perform until his death in 1998.

Did You Know?

- Sam Phillips gave Carl the nickname "Rockabilly Cat."
- "Blue Suede Shoes" was the first Sun record to sell one million copies.
- Elvis also recorded "Blue Suede Shoes," which became one of his signature songs.
- Carl's son, Stan, is also a musician and played in his father's band.
- In 1956, Carl was almost killed in a car wreck while on his way to make his TV debut on *The Perry Como Show*.

Ronnie Hawkins

RONALD HAWKINS was born in Huntsville, in the Arkansas
Ozarks. His birthday, January 10, 1935, was just two days after Elvis
Presley's. When Ronnie was nine years old, his family moved to
nearby Fayetteville. There his father owned a barbershop. It was at
his father's barbershop that he met a black musician named Half
Pint, who became his mentor. When Ronnie graduated from high
school, he enrolled at the University of Arkansas, studying physical
education. It was at the U of A that Ronnie started his own band.

Ronnie Hawkins and the Hawks toured in Oklahoma, Missouri, and Arkansas. They often performed along the Rock 'n' Roll Highway. The group played at Jarvis's and the Silver Moon in Newport. Onstage Ronnie used what he had learned in college studying gymnastics, performing back flips off the stage wall. He entertained the crowds with a dance called the Camel Walk. (Years later Michael Jackson would popularize the same move, calling it the Moonwalk.) Early hits included "Hey, Bo Diddley" and "Suzie Q," written by his cousin, Arkansas native Dale Hawkins.

In 1958 Conway Twitty told Ronnie that he and his band should think about touring Canada. Their first show was a huge success. The group made their first record in a garage in Toronto. In 1964 Ronnie moved to Canada. In time, Ronnie and his band parted ways, but he had found a strong following in Canada and never left.

Ronnie Hawkins has remained a success. In addition to performing his music, he became a successful actor, appearing in films and hosting his own television show. He has survived pancreatic cancer and still lives in Canada. Today, most of his albums have been re-issued on CD.

Did You Know?

- In 2002, Toronto, Canada declared October 4th "Ronnie Hawkins Day," in recognition of his musical career and support of Canadian charities.

- Hawkins toured as an ambassador for peace in John Lennon's "Love Not War" worldwide campaign.

- Ronnie Hawkins received a Juno Award in 1984 as Canada's Best Country Male Vocalist.

- When Ronnie performed in Arkansas he owned the Rockwood Club in Fayetteville. Many early rock 'n' rollers such as Jerry Lee Lewis, Carl Perkins, Conway Twitty, and Roy Orbison entertained there.

- In 1975 Ronnie was chosen by Bob Dylan to play the role of the singer in the film *Renaldo and Clara*.

Joyce Green

JOYCE OLIVIA GREEN was born in 1940 outside of Searcy, Arkansas, in the small town of Bradford. She had one sister and three brothers. Her family was musically talented. She and her siblings sang regularly in church. Her brother Glenn played trumpet in a brass band and also played guitar.

When Joyce was nine years old, she began to learn the guitar. She also started entering local talent contests. Although she had never had guitar or voice lessons, she won many of the contests she entered. Joyce and her siblings started performing at picnics and other events. Soon they were a local attraction.

At age seventeen, Joyce made her radio debut on a station in Searcy. She also began touring in northeast Arkansas, performing along the Rock 'n' Roll Highway, sometimes with rockabilly artists from Sun Studio. A friend introduced her to Arlen Vaden of Vaden Records in Trumann. It was here that Joyce recorded "Black Cadillac," an original song she had written with her sister. Although "Black Cadillac" did not achieve wide distribution or the success many music critics say it deserved, Joyce and her family continued to perform at county fairs and other local events.

By the mid-1970s Joyce had lost interest in pursuing a musical career. Remaining in Bradford, she married and later had a son. Today she still lives in her hometown.

Did You Know?

- Rockabilly artist Teddy Redell said that of all the records he played on, "Black Cadillac" was his favorite.

- As a teenager, Joyce was lucky enough to see Elvis Presley perform two times. This inspired her musical ambitions.

- Joyce toured with Carl Perkins, one of the greatest rockabilly artists.

- Joyce's record, "Black Cadillac," is considered a classic rockabilly song. It is in demand with record collectors and rockabilly fans today.

- Joyce recorded again in the 1970s, but sadly the records were destroyed in a fire.

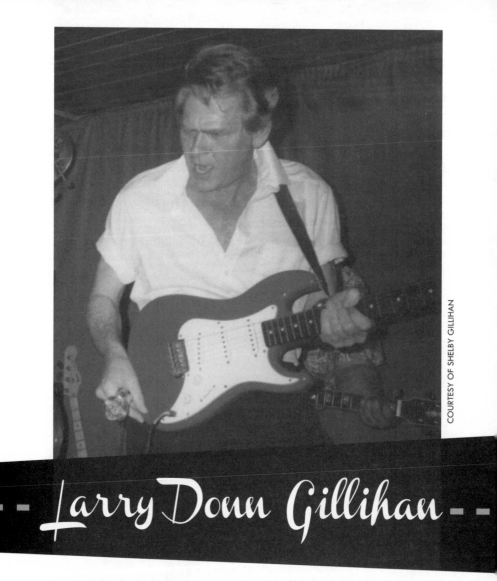

COURTESY OF SHELBY GILLIHAN

Larry Donn Gillihan

LARRY DON GILLIHAN was born in 1941 on his family's farm in Bono, just outside of Jonesboro, Arkansas. He grew up an only child. As a boy, he and his parents listened to country music on the radio. Larry Don sang these songs as he worked in the cotton fields. Like so many other rockabilly performers, Larry Don came from a musical family. In the 1940s one of his uncles played with the Western swing band, Bob Wills and the Texas Playboys.

Larry Don played guitar and piano and also liked to sing. He originally tried to sing like Dean Martin, a swing-era balladeer popular in the 1940s and '50s. But when he saw Sonny Burgess and the Pacers play at the Bono High school gym, he changed his style.

Another exciting event soon occurred at the Bono gym: Elvis performed there. Larry Don was hooked on rockabilly!

Larry Don started his own band when he was sixteen, touring all over northeast Arkansas and southeast Missouri. It was during this time he began performing along Highway 67. He adopted the stage name Larry Donn, dropping his last name and adding a second *n* to his middle name.

In 1957 he met Billy Lee Riley when they were both on the bill for the Craighead County Fair in Jonesboro. That same year, he released his first single with Vaden Records, "That's What I Call a Ball." The flip side was "Honey Bun." When released, they became local favorites.

Larry Donn continued to tour and play music. When rockabilly music became popular again in Europe in the 1980s, he performed at rock 'n' roll festivals nine times. He played shows in Sweden, France, Germany, and England. Today "Honey Bun" and "That's what I Call a Ball," once local favorites, are recognized worldwide.

But Larry Donn accomplished much more than this. He became a radio announcer, news anchor, music columnist, and even owned a music store in Jonesboro. He died in 2012.

Did You Know?

- Larry Donn was expelled from high school for dress-code violation. He wore his collar turned up with his top buttons unbuttoned in the popular style of the day. He earned his diploma through a correspondence course.

- Although he often performed with Bobby Brown and the Curios, Larry Donn wasn't able to play with them in an early tour through Canada. Musicians had to be twenty-one, and he was only seventeen.

- Larry Donn wrote "Honey Bun" in only fifteen minutes because he needed a B-side for his recording of "That's What I Call a Ball."

- Larry Donn learned to play the guitar while recovering from a lawn mower accident. In the accident he lost two toes.

- Larry Donn was probably one of the first Elvis imitators. In 1956 at Bono High School he painted on sideburns with shoe polish and pantomimed to Elvis records.

Bobby Lee Trammell

BOBBY LEE TRAMMELL was born in Jonesboro, Arkansas in 1934. He was raised on a cotton farm with his three brothers and sisters. Bobby Lee was exposed to music from an early age. His parents were both musicians. Bobby Lee and his siblings sang at church. As a young teenager, he learned to play the guitar and would sing at school. He attended a Pentecostal church but would sometimes sneak off to listen to the gospel music being sung at a nearby black church. During his free time, Bobby Lee loved to listen to the *Grand Ole Opry* on the radio.

When Bobby Lee was twenty-two he attended a concert by

Johnny Cash and Carl Perkins at Nettleton High School. He was thrilled when Perkins invited him onstage to perform. After the performance, Perkins encouraged him to go see Sam Phillips. Bobby Lee arrived at Sun Studio with a tape of songs he had written. Phillips was busy and told Bobby Lee to come back in a few weeks. Bobby Lee felt Phillips was brushing him off. Impatient, he went to California and found work in an auto plant while he pursued a recording contract.

In California, Bobby Lee caught the attention of record promoter Fabor Robinson, who signed him to a contract. His first recording, "Shirley Lee," was later covered by Ricky Nelson. Bobby Lee started touring around the United States. But because of his wild and unpredictable performances on stage he began having trouble getting work. Because of this, he decided to move home.

Back in Arkansas, Bobby Lee continued recording on Arkansas record labels such as Vaden Records in Trumann and Ally Records in Jonesboro. During this time, he performed on the Rock 'n' Roll Highway. In 1962 he recorded "Arkansas Twist," which was his biggest hit. In the 1970s he began performing country music.

In the 1990s Bobby Lee became interested in politics and stopped performing. He served in the Arkansas House of Representatives from 1998 to 2002 and died in 2008.

Did You Know?

- Upset that a disk jockey wouldn't play one of his songs, Bobby Lee once climbed to the top of a radio tower to sing the song himself.

- Whenever sales of his records slowed down, Bobby Lee would take them wherever he went and sell them from the trunk of his car.

- Bobby Lee's record "Arkansas Twist" sold around one million copies.

- In the 1960s Bobby Lee went by the nickname "The First American Beatle."

- Bobby Lee never appeared on one of his favorite shows, the *Grand Ole Opry*. Because he behaved so wildly on stage the officials were hesitant to book him.

Jerry Lee Lewis

JERRY LEE LEWIS was born in September 1935 in Ferriday, Louisiana, to Elmo and Mamie Lewis. Being sharecroppers, his family was poor. The family was also very religious and regularly attended church.

When Jerry Lee was eight years old, the untrained boy walked up to his aunt's piano and played "Silent Night" by ear. His parents were so impressed by his talent they mortgaged their home to buy Jerry Lee an old third-hand piano. At age nine he made his debut in church playing "What Will My Answer Be?" While still a teenager, Jerry Lee began playing the local clubs and honky-tonks.

Jerry Lee's mother had other ideas for her son. Mrs. Lewis thought he should be singing for the Lord. She enrolled Jerry Lee at the Southwest Bible Institute, but he did not last long there. He was thrown out for playing a rollicking boogie-woogie version of the gospel song, "My God Is Real."

Like many other performers, Jerry Lee went to Memphis, drawn to Sun Studio and the Memphis sound. In 1956 he became a studio musician and solo artist with Sun. Before his arrival on the scene, Sun artists were seldom accompanied by a piano. Jerry Lee changed all that. His talent was undeniable, and his sound was unique.

In 1957, Lewis broke out as a solo artist with "Whole Lotta Shakin' Goin' On." The song reached the Top Five on the pop, rhythm and blues, and country charts. Other early hits included "Crazy Arms," "Breathless," and Great Balls of Fire."

In the 1960s Jerry Lee transitioned from rock 'n' roll to a career as a successful country performer with hits such as "Another Place, Another Time." But he has never forgotten his early rock 'n' roll roots. Touring today, Jerry Lee is still able to thrill an audience with his early Sun hits.

Did You Know?

- Jerry Lee is the cousin of country singer Mickey Gilley and TV evangelist Jimmy Swaggart. Like Jerry Lee, both play the piano.

- He is nicknamed "the Killer" because of his childhood habit of greeting others by that name.

- Jerry Lee's sister Linda Gail Lewis is a successful pianist and recording star.

- In 2010, *Rolling Stone* magazine named Jerry Lee 24th on its list of 100 Greatest Artists.

- Jerry Lee Lewis is the last surviving member of the "Million Dollar Quartet." This moniker refers to Elvis Presley, Johnny Cash, Carl Perkins, and Jerry Lee, the top money-makers at Sun Records.

Bobby Brown

BOBBY BROWN was born in the small town of Olyphant, Arkansas, just outside Newport, in 1938. His family was musical. He and his two brothers and sisters sang. His father played the guitar, and his mother played a washboard. He and his family loved to listen to the radio. They enjoyed all kinds of music.

One day Bobby heard music he had never heard before. He heard Elvis singing rock 'n' roll. Soon Bobby was singing and playing the guitar rock 'n' roll style at local events along Highway 67. He even had a weekly show on KNBY radio in Newport.

After graduating from high school, Bobby decided to try his luck elsewhere. He moved to St. Louis, started a band, and was soon playing in the area. Quickly tiring of St. Louis, he moved back to Arkansas and settled in Jonesboro, a short distance from Memphis and the rockabilly revolution.

While playing at a nightclub along Highway 67, he was spotted by Arlen Vaden of Vaden Records in Trumann. Vaden released Bobby's songs "Down at Big Mary's House" and "I Get the Blues at Midnight." Other songs soon followed. Bobby continued touring and performing.

After his band broke up, Bobby joined Sonny Burgess and his band. They began touring with Johnny Cash's show, not only along the Rock 'n' Roll Highway but all over the United States. In time, he formed another band, Bobby Brown and the Curios. This group became very popular in Canada.

Today Bobby Brown continues to perform in the United States and overseas.

Did You Know?

- "Down at Big Mary's House" was the first rock 'n' roll song Vaden Records released.

- Bobby performed with other early Rock 'n' Roll Highway entertainers such as Narvel Felts, Wanda Jackson, Conway Twitty, and Larry Donn.

- Bobby wrote "Down at Big Mary's House" with Sonny Burgess.

- Bobby was inducted into the Rockabilly Hall of Fame.

- In the late 1950s Bobby joined Sonny Burgess's band, playing the bass guitar and singing half of the time.

Bud Deckelman

BUD DECKELMAN was born Gene Darrell Deckelman in 1927. This makes him several years older than the other performers rocking along Highway 67. Bud, his four sisters, and three brothers were born and raised in Harrisburg, Arkansas.

As a young man, Bud joined the military. It was there he learned to play the bass guitar. Upon his return to the United States, he moved to Chicago. But by 1954 he was living in Mississippi. Working in Memphis with his brother-in-law, he put up sheetrock during the day. At night, he worked on his music. With his brother Dood, Bud started a band and named it The Daydreamers, after one of their songs, "Daydreamin'."

Bud went to Sun Studio to try to record. Sam Phillips thought he was talented, but he wanted Bud to change his style. Bud didn't want to do that, so he went across town to Meteor Recording Studio and recorded "Daydreamin'." It became a #1 hit in Memphis. It also reached #1 on country charts in several other cities throughout the country.

In 1955 Bud signed a contract with MGM in Nashville. He recorded six singles, but none of them were as popular as "Daydreamin'." Bud toured on the Rock 'n' Roll Highway with such stars as Elvis Presley, Wanda Jackson, and Johnny Cash. Because his style was more country than the other performers, he never achieved their success at a time when rockabilly was sweeping the country. Bud died in 1998.

Did You Know?

- In the 1960s Bud played bass on Eddie Bond's local Memphis television show.
- Because Bud looked and sounded like Hank Williams, he was considered for the lead role in *Your Cheatin' Heart,* a movie about the country singer.
- Bud started his musical career on *The Louisiana Hayride.*
- Bud is the older double cousin of the rockabilly singer Sonny Deckelman.
- Bud had to repair the tape deck at Meteor Records before he could record there.

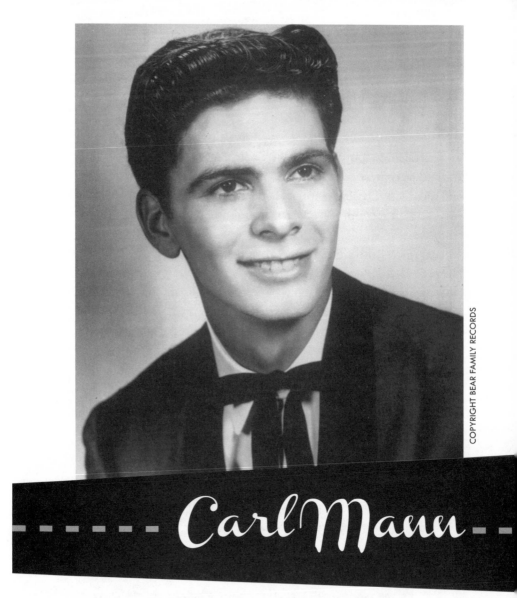

Carl Mann

CARL MANN was born near the town of Huntingdon, Tennessee in 1942. This would make him one of the youngest rockabilly artists to perform along the Rock 'n' Roll Highway. His family owned a lumber business. Carl grew up singing in church and listening to the *Grand Ole Opry*. At eight years old, Carl was playing the guitar, and by ten, he had a regular spot playing on WDXI, a Jackson, Tennessee radio station.

When Carl was just twelve years old he formed his first band. At age thirteen he learned to play the piano. Soon the band was playing in churches and schools. They even played on a radio show called the *Junior Opry* in Nashville.

While Carl was still a teenager he and his band, The Kool Kats, recorded two songs on a small record label named Jaxon. In 1959 Carl signed a contract with Phillips International, Sam Phillips's new record label. In March 1959 Sun released Carl's upbeat arrangement of "Mona Lisa." It was a huge success for the young singer. Mann continued releasing records with Phillips's studio and touring. One of the places he often played was Porky's Rooftop on Highway 67. Although Carl continued to record fine rock 'n' roll material, he never achieved the success of his first release.

In 1964, at the age of twenty-two, Carl was drafted into the army. After he completed his tour of duty, he came home and began performing country music. In 1978 he started touring and recording in Europe. After about ten years, Carl retired from the road, returning to his hometown and his family's logging business.

In 2005, as rockabilly music began to enjoy renewed popularity, Carl came out of retirement and began touring again. He was named to the Rockabilly Hall of Fame in 2006.

Did You Know?

- "Mona Lisa," Carl's first single, reached #25 on the Billboard Hot 100 chart and #24 on the U.S. Black singles chart.

- Carl Mann was Sam Phillips's youngest artist to sell a million records.

- Carl was only sixteen when he recorded "Mona Lisa."

- After hearing the Carl Mann version of "Mona Lisa," Conway Twitty released a similar arrangement with MGM Records. Both versions reached the Billboard Top 50 at the same time. Carl's version outsold Twitty's, but just barely.

- Carl's 1974 hit "Twilight Time" reached #100 on the U.S. Country singles chart.

Charlie Rich

CHARLES RICH was born in Colt, Arkansas in 1932. His parents were cotton farmers. Charlie had two sisters. While growing up, Charlie was exposed to a wide range of music. His father sang in the church gospel quartet. His mother played the piano. The family listened to country music on the radio. Charlie listened to the blues. He was taught to play blues piano by a black sharecropper named C.J. Allen. Later Charlie played saxophone in the Forrest City High School band.

In 1953, Charlie joined the air force. While in the service he formed his first band, The Velvetones. Four years later he returned to Arkansas, moving to Crittenden County. There he farmed during the day and performed music at night. He played local clubs in the Memphis area. He wrote songs with his wife, Margaret Ann.

Living so close to Memphis gave Margaret Ann a good idea. She had heard Elvis Presley and knew he recorded at Sun Studio. So one day she crossed the Mississippi River bridge and took one of Charlie's tapes to Sun Studio. After listening to the tape, Sam Phillips told Margaret Ann that Charlie's style was too jazzy for the Sun sound and that he should try his hand at composing.

Charlie took Phillips's advice and hired on as a session musician. He wrote songs for Johnny Cash, Jerry Lee Lewis, and other Sun Studio artists. Then he began to record his own songs at Sun. It was during this time that Charlie performed on the Rock 'n' Roll Highway to sold-out audiences.

Like many artists of the 1960s, Charlie struggled as musical tastes began to change. He left Sun Records, and in time he found success in the country music field, with such hits as "Behind Closed Doors" and "Most Beautiful Girl" earning him numerous awards. He continued recording and performing, with career ups and downs, until his death in 1995.

Did You Know?

- Charlie's nickname was the "Silver Fox" because of his prematurely white hair.
- In 1973, Charlie and his hit "Behind Closed Doors" received three awards from the Country Music Association: Male Vocalist of the Year, Album of the Year, and Single of the Year.
- A gifted musician, Charlie played the guitar, saxophone, and piano.
- Charlie's wife, Margaret Ann, was the lead singer in his first band.
- Charlie enrolled at Arkansas State College on a football scholarship. Following a football injury he transferred to the University of Arkansas, where he was a member of the marching band.

SOURCES

PRINT SOURCES

Bragg, Rick. *Jerry Lee Lewis: His Own Story.* New York: HarperCollins, 2014.

Davis, Hank. Liner Notes. *Memphis Belles: The Women of Sun Records.* Holste, Germany: Bear Family Records, 2002.

Doyle, Patrick. "The Killer at Peace: Jerry Lee Lewis' Golden Years." *Rolling Stone,* November 4, 2014.

Heard, Kenneth. "Art Festival Helps Shine New Light on Newport." *Arkansas Democrat-Gazette,* February 28, 2015.

Jared, George. "Rockabilly Star Carl Perkins' Son Looks Back on His Father's Career." *Jonesboro Sun,* n.d.

Morrison, Craig. *Go Cat Go: Rockabilly and Its Makers.* Champaign: University of Illinois Press, 1998.

Nelson, Rex. "The Newport Sound." *Arkansas Democrat-Gazette,* October 22, 2014.

Pareles, Jon. "Carl Perkins Dies at 65; Rockabilly Pioneer Wrote 'Blue Suede Shoes." *The New York Times,* January 20, 1998.

Remaklus, Miranda. "Rockabilly Returns to Trumann as Vaden Records is Honored." *Poinsett County Democrat Tribune,* February 12, 2010.

Schwartz, Marvin. *We Wanna Boogie: The Rockabilly Roots of Sonny Burgess and the Pacers.* Little Rock: Butler Center Books, 2014.

INTERVIEWS

Burgess, Sonny. Interviews, March–May, 2015.

Felts, Narvel. Telephone conversation, June 2015.

Weeks, Louise, Interview. June 2015.

WEBSITES

AllMusic, a division of AllMedia Network, LLC. www.allmusic.com

Charlie Rich, The Silver Fox. www.charlierichjr.com/fox/

Conway Twitty. www.conwaytwitty.com

Elvis Presley. www.elvis.com

The Encylopedia of Arkansas History & Culture. Central Arkansas Library System. www.encyclopediaofarkansas.net

Jerry Lee Lewis. www.jerryleelewis.com

Johnny Cash. www.johnnycash.com

Narvel Felts. www.mkoc.com/narvelfelts/

Rock 'N Roll Highway 67 Museum. www.depotdays.org/rock-n-roll-highway-67-museum/

Rockabilly Hall of Fame. www.rockabillyhall.com

Ronnie Hawkins. www.ronniehawkins.com

Sonny Burgess & The Legendary Pacers. www.legendarypacers.com/

Sun Records Company. www.sunrecords.com

Sun Studio. www.sunstudio.com

Teddy Redell. www.TeddyRiedel.com

Wanda Jackson. www.wandajackson.com

ACKNOWLEDGMENTS

A special thanks to Mr. Sonny Burgess for his help during the research and writing of this book, and to my publisher, Liz Smith Russell.

Where would we be without libraries? I owe heartfelt gratitude to the professionals at the Craighead County Library (Jonesboro, Arkansas), the Hernando Public Library (Hernando, Mississippi), and the Llangefni Public Library (Anglesey, Wales).

I would also like to thank the many people who assisted with specific aspects of research and helped us obtain photos of the artists featured in this book: Henry Boyce, Mike Campbell, Patty Trammell Carpenter, Jon Chadwell, Mike Doyle, Narvel Felts, Shelby Gillihan, Peter Hayman, Van Provence, Joni Jenkins Riels, Joyce Riley, David Smock, Louise Weeks, Peggy Wood, and the staff of Bear Family Records.